お稲荷さん

商売繁盛・五穀豊穣の祈願に訪れる神社。全国3万あるお稲荷さんの総本宮が京都の伏見稲荷大社です。

O-Inari-san (Inari shrine)

People visit Inari shrines to pray for prosperity in business or an abundant harvest. There are some thirty thousand Inari shrines throughout the country. Fushimi Inari Taisha, the head shrine, is located in Kyoto.

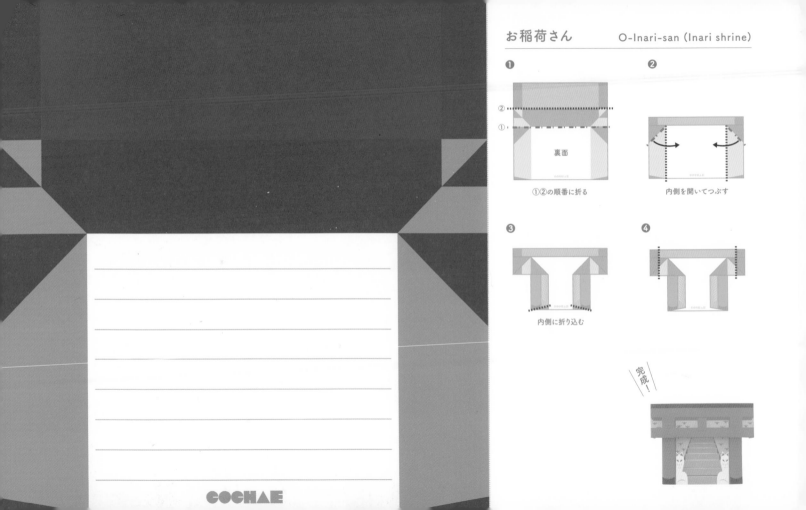

お稲荷さん　O-Inari-san (Inari shrine)

❶

裏面

①②の順番に折る

❷

内側を開いてつぶす

❸

内側に折り込む

❹

完成！

COCHAE

和ろうそく

お寺が多い京都では、ろうそくの需要も多く、その伝統と
技が育まれ美しい和ろうそくが今でも使われています。

Japanese candle

Beautiful Japanese candles, the product of long tradition and
technical skill, are still in use today and in great demand in
Kyoto because of its many temples.

和ろうそく　　Japanese candle

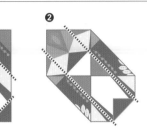

❶
裏面

❷

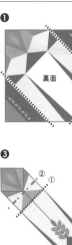

❸
②①
①②の順番に折る

❹
上の紙だけ
内側を開いてつぶす

❺
上の紙だけ
内側を開いてつぶす

❻

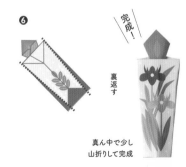

完成！

裏返す

真ん中で少し
山折りして完成

お内裏様

京雛では向かって右側にお内裏様をおきます。これは京都の御所における玉座の位置に基づいています。

O-Dairi-sama

In Kyoto, the Emperor doll displayed on a tiered platform during the Hina Doll Festival, is placed on the right as one faces the platform because it is the same as the position of Emperor's throne in the Imperial Palace in Kyoto.

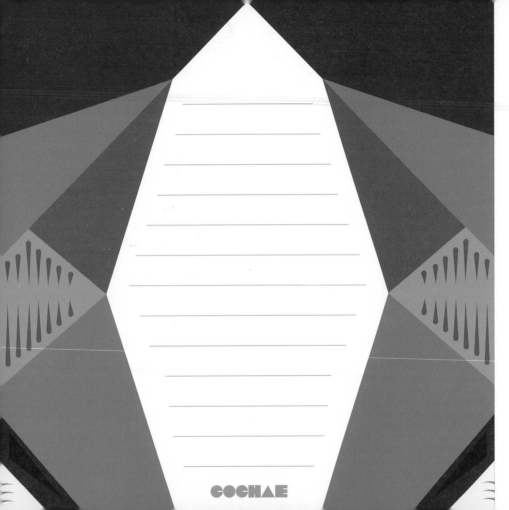

COCHAE

お内裏様　　　　O-Dairi-sama

❶

❷

❸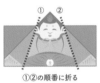

①②の順番に折る

❹

3ヵ所少しだけ折る

完成！

お雛様

ひな祭りはひな人形（お内裏様とお雛様）や桃の花を飾り、
女子のすこやかな成長を祈る節句の行事です。

O-Hina-sama

The Hina Doll Festival is a seasonal event held to wish for
the health and happiness of girls as they grow up. Hina dolls
(Emperor and Empress) are displayed along with decorative
items such as peach blossoms.

お雛様　　　　　　　O-Hina-sama

❶

❷

❸
①②の順番に折る

❹
①②の順番に折る

❺

❻
3ヵ所少しだけ折る

完成！

COCHAE

お琴

日本の和楽器のひとつである琴、日本でその音色が似合う街は？と聞かれたら、答えは京都です。

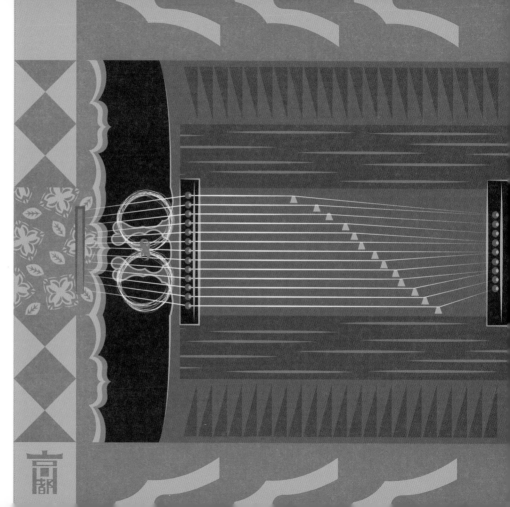

O-koto

The koto is a Japanese musical instrument. If you happen to be asked which city in Japan is a perfect match for the sound of the koto, the answer is "Kyoto!"

お琴　　　　　　　　　　　　　O-koto

❶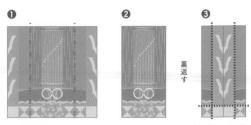

❷

❸

裏返す

折り線をつけて戻す

❹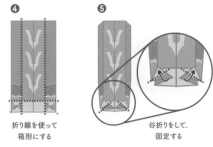

折り線を使って
箱形にする

❺

谷折りをして、
固定する

❻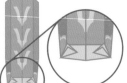

裏返す

完成！

COCHAE

賀茂茄子

京都の上賀茂で 300 年くらいまえからつくられてきた丸なすの一種、京の伝統野菜のひとつです。

Kamo eggplant

Kamo eggplant, a round variety of eggplant grown in the area of Kamigamo in Kyoto for about 300 years, is one of the traditional vegetables of Kyoto.

賀茂茄子   Kamo eggplant

❶
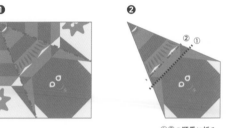

❷

①②の順番に折る

❸

①②③の順番に折る

❹

❺

❻

少し山折り

完成！

絵馬

神社や寺院で、絵柄がついた木の板に合格祈願や恋愛
成就など自分の願いごとを書いて祈願します。

Ema (votive plaque)

Ema are wooden plaques with a picture, usually of a horse or
other animal, found at shrines and temples. People write their
wish on the plaque—for example, success on exams or in love.

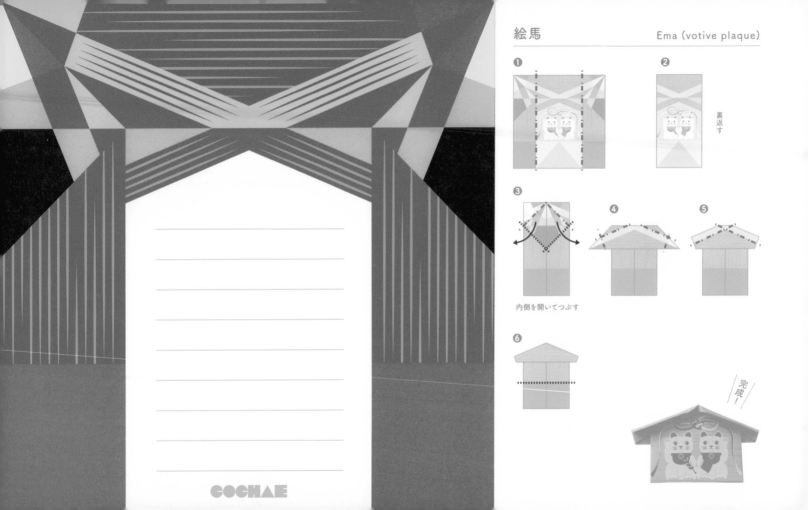

絵馬   Ema (votive plaque)

❶

❷ 裏返す

❸ 内側を開いてつぶす

❹

❺

❻

完成！

きもの

京都の西陣織（先染の紋織物）でつくられた着物は
最高級品で、殿上人のみ着用を許されていました。

Kimono

Kyoto Nishijin (pre-dyed yarn woven into figured fabric) is
a type of elegant kimono of the finest quality, which were
originally worn only by members of the Imperial court and the
aristocracy.

COCHÆ

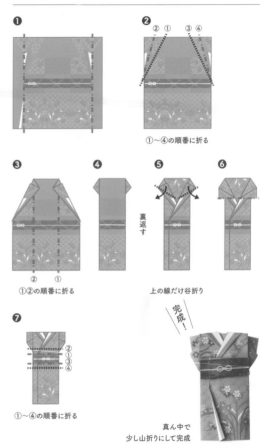

きもの Kimono

❶

❷
②①　③④

①〜④の順番に折る

❸

①②の順番に折る
②①

❹

❺
裏返す

上の線だけ谷折り

❻

❼

①〜④の順番に折る
②①③④

完成！

真ん中で
少し山折りにして完成

股のぞき

京丹後にある日本三景のひとつ天橋立、股の間から逆さの天橋立を見ることを「股のぞき」とよんでいます。

Matanozoki

Amanohashidate sandbar in the city of Kyotango is one of Japan's three most famous scenic spots. The practice of bending down and looking at it through your legs upside down is called matanozoki (peeking through the legs).

股のぞき　　Matanozoki

❶ 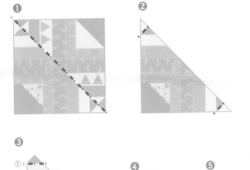 ❷

❸ 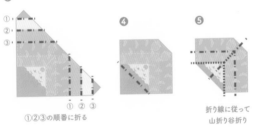 ❹ ❺

①②③の順番に折る

折り線に従って
山折り谷折り

完成！

裏面を折ると
女の子になるよ！

梅

平安初期までは桜よりも知られていて、薬にもなり花見も
できる「梅」が広く人々に愛でられていました。

Plum blossom

The plum blossom was better known than the cherry blossom
up to the early Heian period. It was widely loved both for its
medicinal properties and for its beauty.

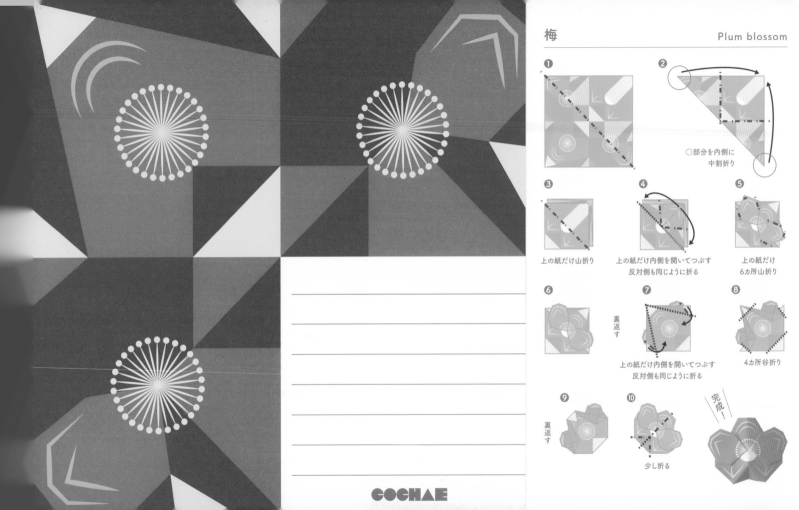

梅

Plum blossom

① **②**

○部分を内側に
中割り折り

③
上の紙だけ山折り

④
上の紙だけ内側を開いてつぶす
反対側も同じように折る

⑤
上の紙だけ
6カ所山折り

⑥
裏返す

⑦
上の紙だけ内側を開いてつぶす
反対側も同じように折る

⑧
4カ所谷折り

⑨
裏返す

⑩
少し折る

完成！

COCHAE

能面

京都では世界無形遺産である能・狂言が定期的に能楽堂や神社の能奉納などで観ることができます。

Noh mask

Noh (classical musical drama) and Kyogen (classical humorous play) have been designated as intangible cultural heritage. In Kyoto, They are regularly performed and can be seen in Noh theaters and also at shrines, where the performances are dedicated to the shrine.

能面 Noh mask

❶

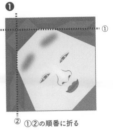

② ①②の順番に折る

❷

❸

❹

上の紙だけ山折り

❺

少しだけ山折り

完成！

COCHAE

扇子

平安時代の京都で扇子は、和歌を読んだり贈答品にしたりと華やかな貴族の儀礼の道具のひとつでした。

Sensu

In the Heian period in Kyoto, people wrote the waka poems they composed on fans (sensu) and gave fans as gifts. Fans were one of the beautiful tools of etiquette of the aristocracy.

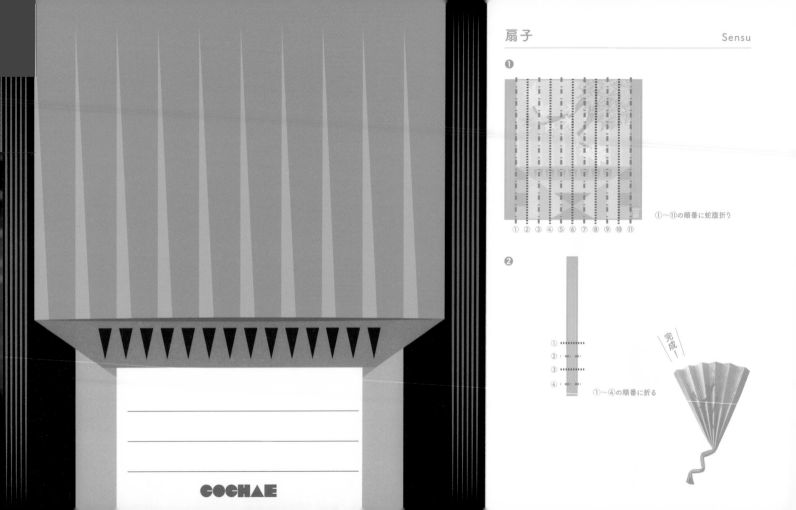

扇子 Sensu

❶

①〜⑪の順番に蛇腹折り

① ② ③ ④ ⑤ ⑥ ⑦ ⑧ ⑨ ⑩ ⑪

❷

①
②
③
④

①〜④の順番に折る

完成！

COCHAE

お坊さん

京都には沢山のお寺があります。お勤めされているお坊さんを街のなかでもお見かけします。

OBOU SAN

Some of the city of Kyoto has a lot of temples, I saw your monk being Otsutome among the town.

お坊さん　　　OBOU SAN

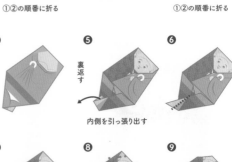

❶ ①②の順番に折る

❷

❸ ①②の順番に折る

❹

❺ 裏返す

内側を引っ張り出す

❻

❼

❽ 4ヵ所折る

❾ 少しだけ山折り

完成！

輪入道

京都の東洞院通りに現れたといわれる車輪の音を立てて道を徘徊する妖怪です。『今昔画図続百鬼』に描かれました。

Wanyudo

Wanyudo, a demon in the form of a flaming face in the middle of an oxcart wheel, is said to appear and prowl through Higashinotoin-dori street in Kyoto making the sound of a cart wheel. An illustration of Wanyudo is found in The Illustrated One Hundred Demons from the Present and the Past.

COCHAE

輪入道　Wanyudo

① 裏面

② 上の紙だけ
折り線にそって折る

③ ○部分も❶❷と
同じように折る

④

⑤

⑥ 上の紙だけ谷折り

⑦

⑧ 上の紙だけ谷折り

⑨

⑩ ○部分を立てて反対側も
❹〜❾と同じように折る

⑪ 裏返す

完成！

鮎

毎年 6 月頃に解禁される鴨川の鮎は、川床の会席で頂いたりと京都の夏の風物詩となっています。

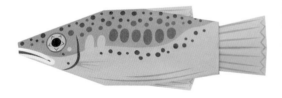

Ayu fish

The ayu fishing season opens every year in June. Eating ayu on an open platform over the bank of Kamo River is a summer tradition in Kyoto.

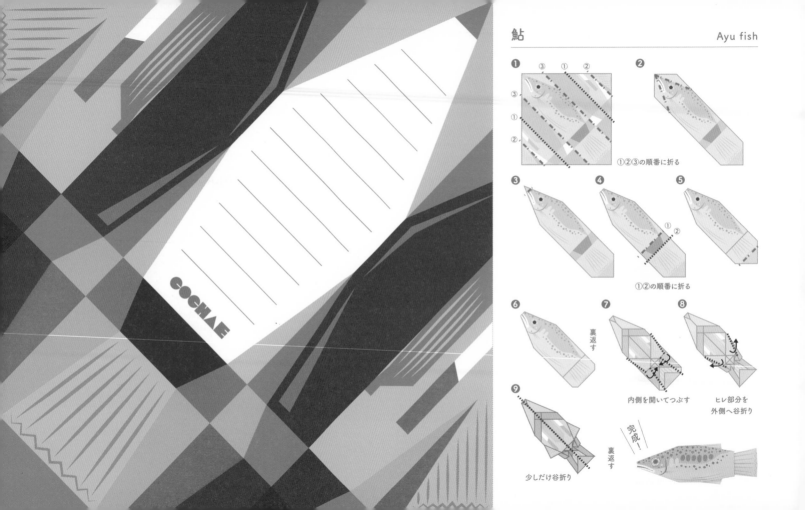

鮎

Ayu fish

❶ ①②③の順番に折る

❷

❸

❹ ①②の順番に折る

❺

❻ 裏返す

❼ 内側を開いてつぶす

❽ ヒレ部分を
外側へ谷折り

❾ 少しだけ谷折り

裏返す

完成！

お地蔵さん

平安京の時代から現代まで、京都の街の暮らしのなかで祀られ地域の人々を守られているお地蔵さんです。

O-Jizo-san

From times of old when Kyoto was the ancient capital of Japan up to the present day, O-Jizo-san has been worshipped in the course of daily life in Kyoto as a beloved divinity who protects both living people and the souls of the dead.

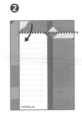

お地蔵さん　　　　　　　　　O-Jizo-san

❶

①②の順番に折る

❷

内側を開いてつぶす

❸

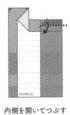

①②の順番に折る

❹

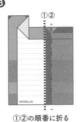

内側を開いてつぶす

❺

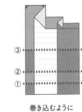

巻き込むように
①②③の順番に折る

❻

裏返す

4カ所山折り

完成！

COCHAE

抹茶ソフトクリーム

京都といえば、抹茶が有名で沢山のお茶席があります。
手軽に楽しめる抹茶ソフトクリームも大人気です。

Macha soft serve ice cream

Speaking of Kyoto, finely powdered green tea called macha
is a familiar part of life there. It's used in tea ceremonies,
which are frequently held. Macha soft serve ice cream is an
easy, informal way to enjoy the flavor of macha.

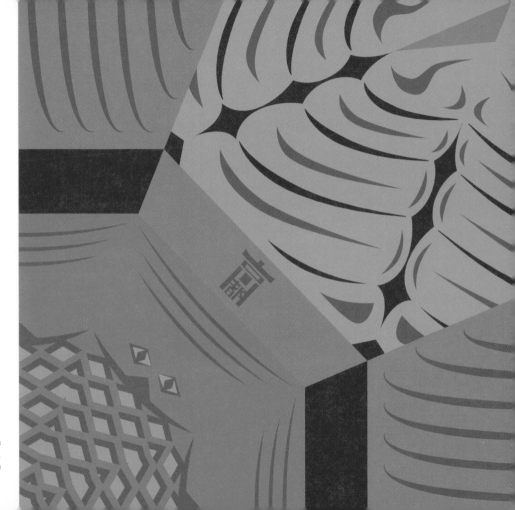

抹茶ソフトクリーム　Macha soft serve ice cream

❶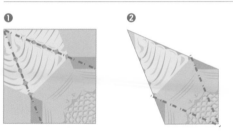

❷

❸

❹

❺

①②の順番に折る

3カ所山折り

少しだけ山折り

完成！

COCHAE

お寺

古都京都には、世界遺産登録されているお寺が沢山あり、
国内外からの観光客でいつも賑わっています。

O-Tera

Many temples constructed long ago when Kyoto was the
ancient capital of Japan, are registered as a World Heritage.
Nowadays the temple grounds are lively with tourists from
Japan and foreign countries.

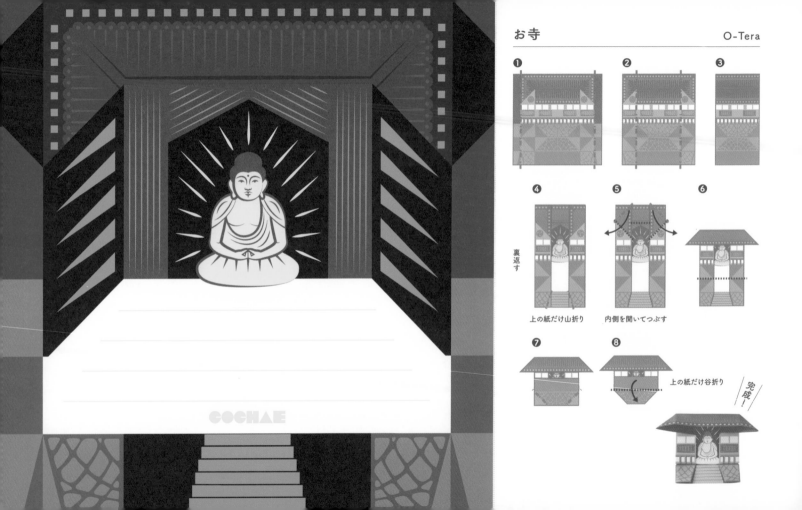

お寺　　　　　　　　　　　　　O-Tera

❶❷❸

❹ 裏返す　　上の紙だけ山折り

❺ 内側を開いてつぶす

❻

❼

❽ 上の紙だけ谷折り

完成！

COCHAE

大文字

五山の送り火は、お盆にこの世に帰ってきた精霊を、あの世に
お見送りする京都の行事です。

Daimonji

Gozan no Okuribi (five mountain bonfires) is a festival in
Kyoto held to send off the spirits of the dead that are
believed to visit this world during the Obon season.

大文字　　　　Daimonji

❶

❷
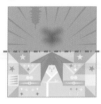

○部分を内側に中割り折り

❸
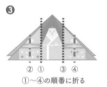

②①　③④
①〜④の順番に折る

❹

内側に折り込む

❺

❻

内側を少し広げる

完成！

大天狗

京都の奥座敷・鞍馬山に住んでいたと伝えられている天狗。牛若丸（源義経）に剣術などを教えたとされています。

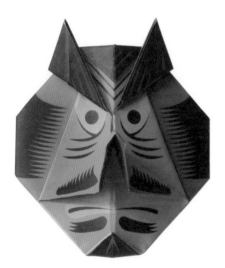

Dai -Tengu

Tradition has it that the Great Tengu lived in Mount Kurama in the far north of Kyoto. He is said to have taught the art of swordsmanship to Ushiwakamaru (Minamoto no Yoshitsune).

大天狗 Dai -Tengu

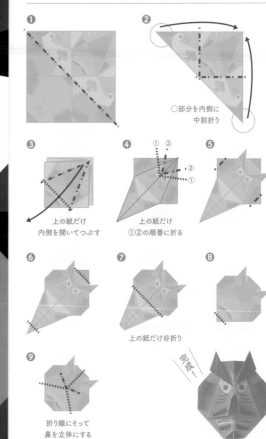

①

②
○部分を内側に
中割り折り

③
上の紙だけ
内側を開いてつぶす

④
① ②
上の紙だけ
①②の順番に折る

⑤

⑥

⑦
上の紙だけ谷折り

⑧

⑨
折り線にそって
鼻を立体にする

完成!!

貝合わせ

平安時代から伝わる遊びで、貝のなかに左右でひとつになる文字や絵を描いて合わせて遊びます。

Kai-awase (paired clamshells)

A game handed down from the Heian period in which the left and right halves of shells are paired by matching the picture or letters painted on the shells.

COCHAE

貝合わせ　Kai-awase (paired clamshells)

❶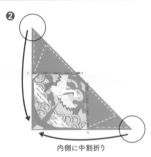

❷

内側に中割折り

❸

折りスジをつける

❹

折りスジを使って
折り線に沿って立体にする

❺

3ヵ所山折り

完成！

裏面を折ると
亀が出てくるよ！

舞妓さん

京都・祇園の花街で、舞踊やお囃子をお座敷にて披露する芸妓さんを目指す人です。

Maiko-san (apprentice geisha)

In Gion, the geisha quarter of Kyoto, apprentice geisha called maiko study to someday perform the traditional dance to musical accompaniment and other forms of entertainment performed by geisha.

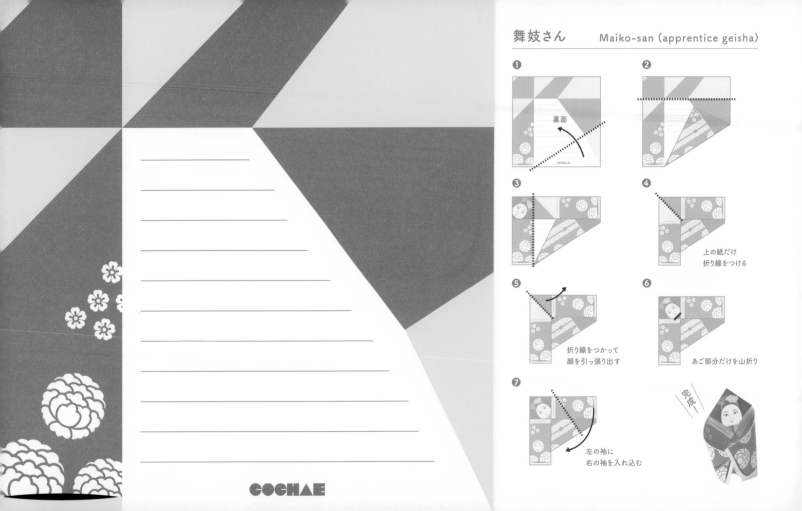

舞妓さん　Maiko-san (apprentice geisha)

❶ 裏面

❷

❸

❹ 上の紙だけ
折り線をつける

❺ 折り線をつかって
顔を引っ張り出す

❻ あご部分だけを山折り

❼ 左の袖に
右の袖を入れ込む

完成！

COCHAE

落雁

様々な型と色とりどりにつくられた京都らしいお菓子のひとつ、お茶席の干菓子としても使われます。

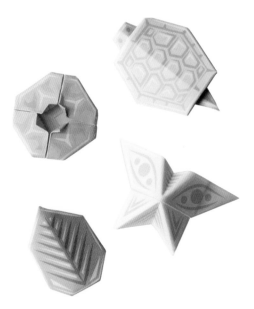

RAKUGAN

One of the various types and Kyoto seems candy made in colorful, it is also used as a dry confectionery of tea ceremony.

落雁　　　　　　　　　RAKUGAN

柿

❶

 裏面

十字線にそって切る

❷

❸

葉

❶ 　**❷** 　**❸** 　**❹**

少し山折り

亀

❶
①

②

❷
⑤④③

①②

❸

①②の順番に折る　①②の順番に折る　少し山折り

蝶

❶ 　**❷** 　**❸**

上の紙だけ
開いてつぶす

❹

完成！

お内裏さま
O-Dairi-sama

お内裏さまの折り方を見ながら、
折ってみよう！ 描いてみよう！
自分だけのオリジナル折紙をつくろう！

Look at the O-Dairi-sama drawing on the previous page
to fold and draw!
Make your very own origami art!

お雛さま
O-Hina-sama

お雛さまの折り方を見ながら、
折ってみよう！ 描いてみよう！
自分だけのオリジナル折紙をつくろう！

Look at the O-Hina-sama drawing on the previous page
to fold and draw!
Make your very own origami art!

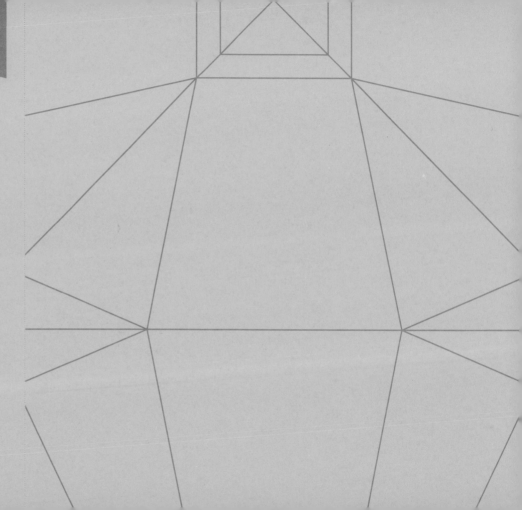

絵馬
Ema (votive plaque)

絵馬の折り方を見ながら、
折ってみよう！ 描いてみよう！
自分だけのオリジナル折紙をつくろう！

Look at the Ema drawing on the previous page
to fold and draw!
Make your very own origami art!

能面
Noh mask

能面の折り方を見ながら、
折ってみよう！ 描いてみよう！
自分だけのオリジナル折紙をつくろう！

Look at the Noh mask drawing on the previous page
to fold and draw!
Make your very own origami art!

大文字
Daimonji

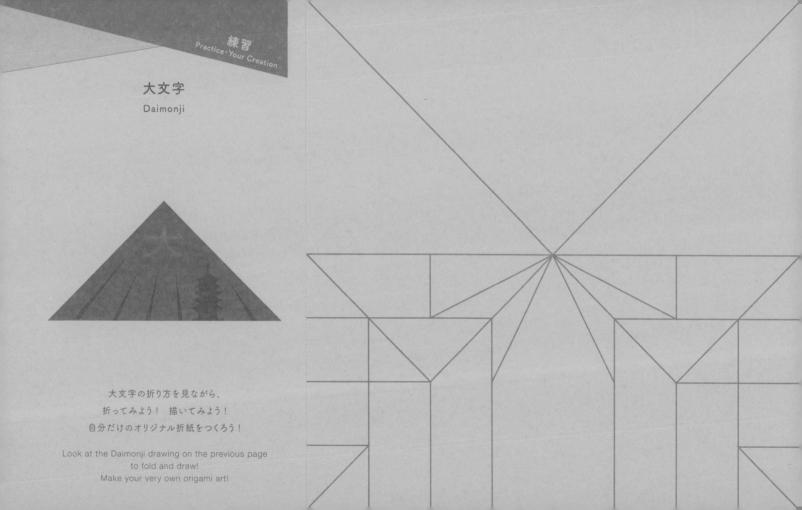

大文字の折り方を見ながら、
折ってみよう！ 描いてみよう！
自分だけのオリジナル折紙をつくろう！

Look at the Daimonji drawing on the previous page
to fold and draw!
Make your very own origami art!

貝合わせ
Kai-awase (paired clamshells)

貝合わせの折り方を見ながら、
折ってみよう！ 描いてみよう！
自分だけのオリジナル折紙をつくろう！

Look at the Kai-awase drawing on the previous page
to fold and draw!
Make your very own origami art!

舞妓さん

Maiko-san (apprentice geisha)

舞妓さんの折り方を見ながら、
折ってみよう！　描いてみよう！
自分だけのオリジナル折紙をつくろう！

Look at the Maiko-san drawing on the previous page
to fold and draw!
Make your very own origami art!

お地蔵さん

O-Jizo-san

お地蔵さんの折り方を見ながら、
折ってみよう！ 描いてみよう！
自分だけのオリジナル折紙をつくろう！

Look at the O-Jizo-san drawing on the previous page
to fold and draw!
Make your very own origami art!